This
BUSINESS PLANNER
Belongs To

....

....

....

it's in the **DOING**, not just the **THINKING**, that we accomplish **OUR GOALS.**

BRAINSTORMING SHEET

What are you good at?

What do you love to make or do for fun?

What other people think you're good at?

BRAINSTORMING SHEET

What do you enjoy doing in your spare time?

What are some of your favorite things?

What things do you enjoy collecting?

BUSINESS PLAN
IDEA

1.

2.

3.

4.

5.

6.

7.

8.

BUSINESS PLAN
WHAT'S IN?

Draw your business logo

Slogan

| Business Theme | Business Colors | Pricelist | Business Goals |

BUSINESS PLAN
SERVICES OFFERED

A — IDEA

Describe what service are you offering:

How often do you provide this service?

Why did you choose this service?

Will someone be helping you provide this service?

B — TARGET MARKET

Target Customers:

Location:

Demographics:

C — PRICING

D — COMPETITORS

Do you have competitors?

What makes your service different from others?

E — MARKETING STRATEGY

What will be your edge?

BUSINESS PLAN
MY PRODUCT

BUSINESS

- **Describe your business** _____
- **Product** _____
- **Description of your product** _____
- **Business Goals** _____
- **Business Notes** _____

TARGET MARKET

- **Customers** _____
- **Location** _____

COST

- **Where to get It?** _____
- **Pricing** _____
- **Theme** _____
- **Are you hiring?** _____

COMPETITORS

_____

_____

MARKETING STRATEGY

_____

_____

_____

_____

ONLINE BUSINESS
CLICK and SELL

DOMAIN NAME

BUSINESS DESCRIPTION

PRODUCT / SERVICE

TARGET MARKET

COMPETITORS

WEBSITE INFO

MARKETING STRATEGY

BUSINESS IDEA BREAKDOWN

MATERIALS NEEDED

MATERIALS I ALREADY HAVE

WHERE AND HOW COULD I ADVERTISE FOR THIS BUSINESS

POTENTIAL CUSTOMERS ALREADY INTERESTED IN THIS SERVICE OR PRODUCT

MATERIALS NEEDED
CHECKLIST

✓	Materials Needed	Own / Buy
☐		
☐		
☐		
☐		
☐		
☐		
☐		
☐		
☐		
☐		
☐		

PLACES TO ADVERTISE

PLACE	PRICE

Total Advertisement Cost

BUSINESS
TO-DO LIST

To Buy

○ _____
○ _____
○ _____
○ _____
○ _____
○ _____
○ _____

To Make / Create

○ _____
○ _____
○ _____
○ _____
○ _____
○ _____
○ _____

Appointments

○ _____
○ _____
○ _____
○ _____
○ _____
○ _____
○ _____

To Learn

○ _____
○ _____
○ _____
○ _____
○ _____
○ _____
○ _____

BUSINESS
TO-DO LIST

Other
- _____
- _____
- _____
- _____
- _____
- _____
- _____

Other
- _____
- _____
- _____
- _____
- _____
- _____
- _____

Other
- _____
- _____
- _____
- _____
- _____
- _____
- _____

Other
- _____
- _____
- _____
- _____
- _____
- _____
- _____

YEARLY BUSINESS GOALS

January	February	March

April	May	June

July	August	September

October	November	December

BUSINESS TASK SCHEDULE

DATE	TASK	✓

BUSINESS EXPENSES
TRACKER

DATE	EXPENSE NAME	COST	TOTAL EXPENSE

BUSINESS INCOME TRACKER

DATE	PRODUCT / SERVICE COMPLETED	AMOUNT	TOTAL INCOME

BUSINESS PROFIT TRACKER

MONTH	INCOME	EXPENSES	TOTAL PROFIT
January			
February			
March			
April			
May			
June			
July			
August			
September			
October			
November			
December			

Total Yearly Profit

BUSINESS PROFIT PLAN

How will you spend the business profits?

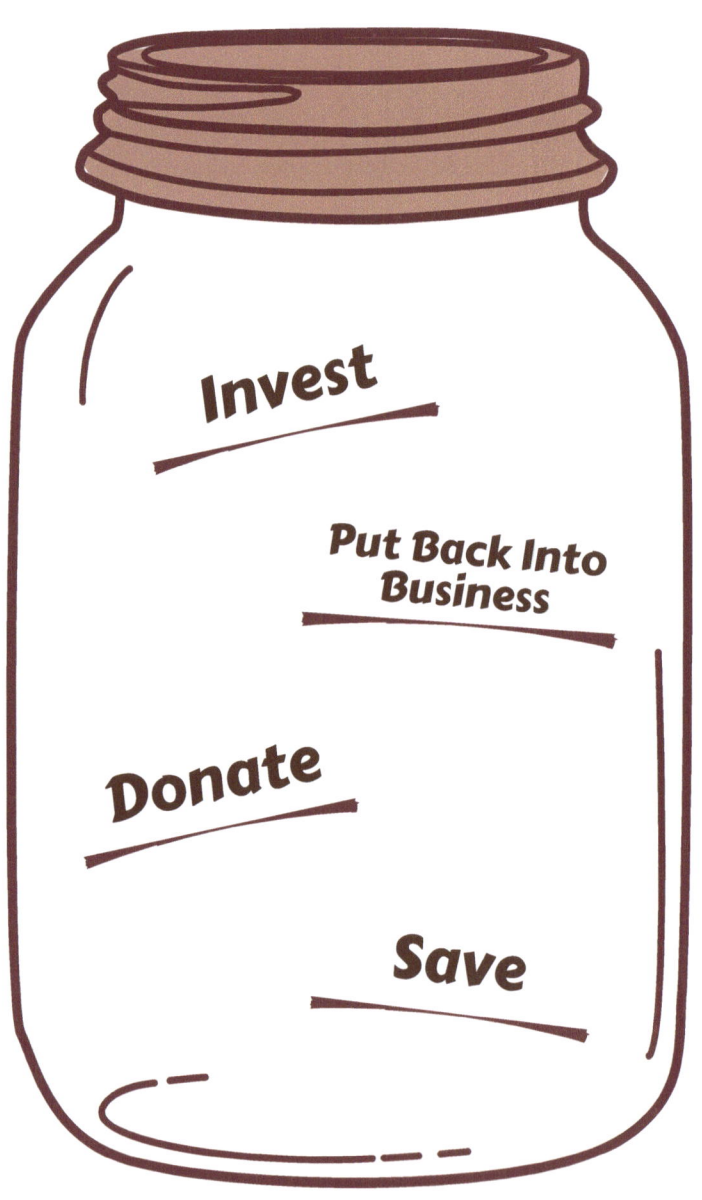

- Invest
- Put Back Into Business
- Donate
- Save

BUSINESS NOTES

BUSINESS NOTES

Copyright© 2022 by Bookfly Publishing

No part of this publication may be reproduced, stored in a retrieval system, or transmitted in any form or by any means, electronic, mechanical, photocopying, recording, or otherwise, without the written permission of the publisher. Limited Liability/Disclaimer of Warranty. The publisher and the author make no representation or warranties with the respect to the accuracy or completeness of the contents of this work and specifically disclaim all warranties including without limitation warranties for a particular purpose. No warranty may be created or extended by sales or promotional materials. The advice or strategies contained herein may not be suitable for every situation. This work is sold with the understanding that the publisher is not engaged in rendering medical, legal, or other professional advice or services. Neither the publisher nor the author or creator shall be liable for damages arising.

For general information on our other products and services please visit www.bookflypublishing.com or contact us at info@bookflypublishing.com.
Bookfly Publishing publishes its books and materials in a variety of electronic and print formats. Some content that appears in print may not be available in electronic books and vice versa.

ISBN 978-1-7369393-9-0
All rights reserved. Published by Bookfly Publishing
Harvey, Louisiana
www.bookflypublishing.com

Printed in the USA

www.ingramcontent.com/pod-product-compliance
Lightning Source LLC
Chambersburg PA
CBHW050747110526
44590CB00003B/106